ABANDONED SOUTH ARKANSAS

NATURAL STATE, NATURAL DECAY

GINGER BECK

AMERICA THROUGH TIME®
ADDING COLOR TO AMERICAN HISTORY

America Through Time is an imprint of Fonthill Media LLC
www.through-time.com
office@through-time.com

Published by Arcadia Publishing by arrangement with Fonthill Media LLC
For all general information, please contact Arcadia Publishing:
Telephone: 843-853-2070
Fax: 843-853-0044
E-mail: sales@arcadiapublishing.com
For customer service and orders:
Toll-Free 1-888-313-2665

www.arcadiapublishing.com

First published 2019

ISBN 978-1-63499-193-3

Typeset in Trade Gothic 10pt on 15pt
Printed and bound in England

CONTENTS

ACKNOWLEDGMENTS

Throughout my adventures in exploring, many people have made the process possible. Thanks so much to my parents, Ron and Becky Beck; my daughter, Jane Claire Beck; some of my partners in exploring: Brianna Pennington, Zach Griffith, Janet Jennings, Brian Halley, Michael Schwarz, and Andrew Breedlove; property owners and memory tellers such as Cynthia Polk, Imie Noble Carpenter, Sheryl Gilliam, and the good people of Ashley and Chicot Counties.

All photographs were taken by the author unless otherwise noted.

This book is dedicated to Aaron Rice.
Our hearts are as empty as these places without you.

INTRODUCTION

I'm a Southern girl. I was born in Memphis, but raised in the Mississippi Delta. I grew up with a deep ditch and soybean fields in my backyard. I never realized lots of people bought ground beef from the grocery store, because we used deer meat for burgers, spaghetti, and my favorite special dish: Hamburger Helper. When I was fifteen, my family moved to South Arkansas, and I discovered there were places even more rural and more southern than Greenville. Hamburg, Arkansas, had around 3000 people at the time, and I thought my life was over. There were only three red lights and not even a Sonic in 1995. It didn't take me long, however, to form friendships and a love for the whole area. My mother worked in Wilmot, and that was even smaller than Hamburg. My whole life was a series of driving past cotton fields, rice fields, and soybean fields. There was something beautiful in the symmetry of it. I began to catch sight of places that were empty—homes and buildings that were boarded up or with broken windows and open doors. I wanted to see inside. I wanted to *know*. What made the South special? What made the Blues get its flavor? What made people get glassy eyed and smile wistfully when reminiscing?

Eventually, I grew up and moved myself and my daughter to Little Rock; I continued my teaching career and began dabbling in all sorts of hobbies: singing, airstreaming, tattooing, photography, and finally, exploring. When I realized the southern part of the state was a gold mine for abandoned places, I began documenting them and researching their history for our website: www.AbandonedAR.com.

The posts were a hit online. So many nice people began telling their memories about each place, thanking me for remembering days gone by and even a little sad seeing their old stomping grounds crumbling and covered in moss. Seeing how much my photos meant to people, I decided to cover as many remote and forgotten places as I could. Word of mouth is powerful, and I soon realized just how many places were hidden where I had been by hundreds of times.

I hope you enjoy this sample of places, as there are still so many hidden gems among the trees and fields. I haven't forgotten, and I hope documenting some in this book will keep these structures alive even after the bricks are all overgrowth covered and the final roof has come down.

Note: Any mistakes in dates or history are mine, as word of mouth and some stories vary when information isn't readily available. My heart is in the right place.

Jerome War Relocation Center

Lake Village

Dermott

Right: Crossett

Below: Lake Village

Above: Wilmot

Left: Eudora

1

ROSS VAN NESS

The little community of Ross Van Ness never made huge headlines, but the school became a landing spot for some students after a national headline fueled by racial tension in the nearby town of Eudora.

Ross Van Ness School

Stories vary about what happened on April 21, 1976, at Eudora High School; however, when the bell rang that morning, nobody went inside the building. Some said it started as an argument over a girl the previous evening, but regardless, tensions between black and white students erupted in an explosive fight that lasted around thirty minutes and changed the course of the town's history.

Integration had gone relatively smoothly for the first five years or so; this was an accomplishment considering the long and sordid history of racism in the area and the South as a whole. But after the riot, state police intervened; a curfew was set, and the superintendent and the school board voted to close the schools for the remaining five weeks of the year due to the "insurmountable difficulties" that occurred and undoubtedly would continue. Perhaps the problems could have been settled with the help of community leaders after some cool-down time, but instead, all the high school's white teachers and many of the white students had the excuse, opportunity, and time to leave, which resulted in what was essentially the re-segregation of the town's schools. For Eudora, it was the beginning of a long period of population decline and economic suffering.

Ross Van Ness School

Ross Van Ness School

Ross Van Ness School

After the riot at Eudora High School in 1976, the Ross Van Ness School was inundated with new white students and made great efforts to expand to accommodate the new enrollment.

On July 1, 1985 the Ross Van Ness School District consolidated into the Eudora School District.

The building today remains a waterlogged shell, with only a few chairs and attendance records left behind.

Ross Van Ness School

Ross Van Ness School

People have fond memories of Ross Van Ness:

My brother and I both attended Ross Van Ness, 1947-1955 and 1955-1963, respectively. It only went through the eighth grade at that time, then we had to transfer to Eudora High School. My memories of Ross Van Ness could not be any sweeter. I can still see the teachers, principals, cafeteria workers, bus drivers, classmates and friends, the classrooms, office, auditorium, gym and grounds of that special place. Ross Van Ness may have been small in size, but it was big in stature. It will always hold a special place in my heart with special memories. It was there that I received a solid educational foundation, one that I was able to expand on twenty-two years later. I will never forget!

Betty McDill

Ross Van Ness School

> I remember playing basketball there in junior high. We drove and drove through miles of farmland then suddenly we were there, as if it just materialized out of thin air.
>
> Pollyanna Burt

While many schools that were part of integration still stand, smaller schools that felt effects of segregation, integration, re-segregation, and re-integration, such as little Ross Van Ness, are left behind. The attendance records and children's chairs are some of the only evidence that young minds were once educated there on the small country road.

Ross Van Ness School

Ross Van Ness School

Ross Van Ness School

Ross Van Ness School

2

PARKDALE HIGH SCHOOL

In Ashley County, there are many small communities, once hubs of activity, which are now gently sleeping. No school bells ring in Parkdale anymore; students go to Hamburg, or Lake Village, among others. The community is a tiny one, home to approximately 150 people, but the area and those surrounding it are rich with history.

In the early twentieth century, the small population of Parkdale became notorious for violent crimes, including murders. Historian Y. W. Ethridge described Parkdale as a "'boisterous community' due to the railroad, sawmills, and saloons." One citizen later said, "Parkdale was terrible. There were a bunch of outlaws. It was a shoot-up town ... There was a rough and rowdy white element here. It was wild."

Today it is a tiny, quiet little area, with no similarity to its wild past: no saloons, and not even a gas station.

Parkdale High School

Parkdale High School

The Parkdale High School building is still standing, albeit extremely damaged, especially the roof, allowing nature to grow inside the cinderblock walls where students once learned their lessons. The gym building, however, is dry and intact, unlike the school with its spongy moss-covered floors and blackboards, a few toppled desks, and broken toilets.

After desegregation, the nearby Savage High School was integrated with Parkdale High School until its last school year in 1993-1994, when it consolidated with Hamburg School District.

Parkdale High School

Parkdale High School

Parkdale High School [*Briana Pennington*]

Parkdale High School

Parkdale High School

Parkdale High School

3

DR. ROBERT GEORGE WILLIAMS HOUSE

Dr. Robert George Willliams House, Parkdale

Dr. Robert George Willliams House, Parkdale

Traveling through Ashley County on the way to Wilmot or Eudora, if you blink, you'll not only miss this house, but you'll miss the entire community of Parkdale, described previously. However, despite the tiny population around it, this grand home has caught the eye of Highway 8 travelers for over 100 years.

For years, I drove past this house, like many others have before and after me, and just called it "the big white house." I always knew it was impressive and beautiful. I was lucky enough to get permission from the current owners to go inside and see it. Although it has been in decline for some years, it still has so much life in it, and I can't wait to see someone renovate it.

The Dr. Robert George Williams House was listed on the National Register of Historic Places in 1984. It was built in 1903 for Dr. Robert George Williams, a prominent medical doctor and businessman in Ashley County, and it is one of the most elaborately decorated houses and arguably the most memorable home in Parkdale. In its beginning, it was a simple wood-frame gable end house with a porch across the front, but it was extensively altered in 1917, giving it the Colonial Revival flair it has today.

Occupying a larger corner lot, the house has always had novelty siding and rests upon brick piers. The two gabled additions were added to both the side and the rear elevation. A two-story flat-roofed three-sided portico was added to the front which greatly changed the exterior. Seven fluted Doric columns support the portico that extends into a *porte cochère* on the east elevation. The second floor of the porch has a railing of decorative slats, still decorated with large colored Christmas lights from years past; it is sagging and unstable, but can one day be grand again with the right owner and some TLC.

The home is currently privately owned by residents in Ashley County; they are greatly interested in renovation, although they are attempting to sell at the time this book was being sent to press.

Dr. Robert George Willliams House, Parkdale

Dr. Robert George Willliams House, Parkdale

Dr. Robert George Willliams House, Parkdale

Dr. Robert George Willliams House, Parkdale

Dr. Robert George Willliams House, Parkdale

Dr. Robert George Willliams House, Parkdale

Dr. Robert George Willliams House, Parkdale

Dr. Robert George Willliams House, Parkdale

4

FIRST PRESBYTERIAN CHURCH OF FORDYCE

The First Presbyterian Church of Fordyce is important both for the history of its congregation and the significance of its talented designer.

The First Presbyterian Church was organized in August of 1883, when a church bell was presented to the congregation by Colonel Fordyce of St. Louis, Missouri. It was the first church organized within the city limits of the new town and subsequently named in Colonel Fordyce's honor. Founded with only six charter members, the congregation had increased to 88 by 1899, first occupying a white frame building which sat at the corner of Third and Oak Streets.

After selling this building to the Christian Church, the First Presbyterian congregation met in a brick building located at Fifth and Main Streets. The third and present church, pictured here, was built in 1912. Designed by Reuben Harrison Hunt (1362-19371, a noted architect from Tennessee), the First Presbyterian Church is a well-preserved example of this important designer's ecclesiastical work.

First Presbyterian Church of Fordyce

Considered one of Tennessee's most significant architects, Hunt was the subject of a thematic nomination to the National Register in 1979 prepared by the Tennessee Historic Commission. Hunt most frequently designed churches, educational and public buildings, often in the Gothic Revival style. Though he had little formal architectural training, he designed his first major project, the First Baptist Church in Chattanooga, at age twenty-four. From that time on, Hunt designed numerous brick and stone churches throughout the South, of which the First Presbyterian Church is representative.

The current organization owning the church was kind enough to let me in to document the lovely old building, still decorated from a long-ago Christmas past. It was so interesting to see the remains of days gone by, especially in the nursery, which was set up as if last Sunday children were rocked and sung to and next Sunday was right around the corner.

The building was listed on the National Register of Historic Places in 1983.

First Presbyterian Church of Fordyce

First Presbyterian Church of Fordyce

First Presbyterian Church of Fordyce

5

SUNSET DRIVE-IN AND ROLLER RINK

Sunset Drive-In, Hamburg [*courtesy Robert A. Carpenter, Jr.*]

First kisses, buzzing mosquito coils, and sneaking into movies in cars: these are several of countless memories of the Sunset Drive-In theater and the Sunset Roller Rink in Hamburg, Arkansas, a small town of around 3,000 people in the heart of Southeast Arkansas.

According to Mrs. Imie Carpenter in *Reflections of Ashley County*, the drive-in was built on land south of Hamburg purchased by Charles F. Carpenter, Sr. and was constructed by his sons, Charles and Jack. Sadly, Charles was killed in a 1954 plane crash. Charles' widow, Marjorie, and his brother, Jack, sold the property to Robert Allen Carpenter, who had returned home from service in Korea and continued the operation of the theater. Years later, Robert's wife, Imie, and son, Robert Allen Carpenter, Jr. joined in helping with the theater also. The roller rink was also owned (and still is owned to this day) and operated by Robert A. and Imie. The first rink was a massive tent-like structure, later replaced by the existing wooden building. It was open on Friday and Saturday night for skating and events such as birthday parties.

Today it remains. Tall pine trees now cover the parking area, once shaped like a baseball field with seemingly endless rows for parking next to speakers on poles. A short step into the wooded area leads to the skating rink, an open-air wooden structure with a wooden floor, which no doubt used to be slick for wheels to fly across. The beams above and the structural poles still stand strong. The outside is still emblazoned with white and yellow paint: *Sunset Roller Rink*.

Walking deeper into the woods, visitors may find the occasional overturned speaker pole, but remnants of anything other than woods are rare—that is, until suddenly a giant white triumph of wooden movie screen comes into view. Truly a testament to hard work and solid building, it stands with pride, held in place by massive beams. No trees or weather has torn it down. If a movie were projected on it today, it undoubtedly would only appear slightly aged.

A short walk away from the screen leads to a now defunct concession stand and bathroom area made of cinderblock, no doubt the site of many hot dogs, bags of popcorn, and fountain sodas purchased and consumed.

Sunset, Hamburg

Sunset Roller Rink, Hamburg

Sunset Roller Rink, Hamburg

Sunset Roller Rink, Hamburg

With the decline in the novelty of American drive-in theaters, it is our wish to highlight and remember this amazing structure, no doubt the hot spot of a small town, filled with memories that many people still fondly recount today:

> My husband and I had our first date at the drive-in and then spent many weekends at the skating rink. There was a big sign that announced what was playing on the north corner. It had a little room that held all the letters. Many couples would go to the sign room to make out.
>
> Sandra Oliver

> I went with my mom and younger brother to see *Animal House* there. I had heard about it and refused to stay in the car and watch it with her. I watched it from the metal chairs just outside the snack bar. My younger brother stayed in the car and was PO'd because he couldn't laugh out loud at anything. Mom was horrified.
>
> Paul Selby

> Skated many a mile in there with Shawn, who was four. I remember me and Carolyn taught Bobbie Wright to skate in there; he like to have killed us 'till he learned how. Never say a one-legged man can't skate!
>
> Marilyn J Bates

Right: Sunset Roller Rink, Hamburg

Below: Sunset Drive-In, Hamburg

Sunset Drive-In, Hamburg

Went to that drive-in there lots of times! My first date was at Sunset Drive-In with my husband of fifty-three years! In 1963 we started dating! *Bird man of Alcatraz* was playing! What memories! Would load kids in trunk and go! Had fun!

Patti Wright Hilborn

I worked there with Larry Myers and Kay Lynn Cox. We worked at the drive-in as well as the skating rink. It was 1979 through 1982 when I graduated. Mr. Bobby would drive that big long Cadillac to pick us up before work, and afterwards he would take us all home. We also would have swimming parties at their house sometimes after we closed the skating rink. I do know for sure that Mr. Bobby did all the posters on the snack bar walls. He was a very talented artist. He also had a temper to blow all tempers! I loved them both, always will remember good times there. He paid us $1 an hour and all the popcorn and coke we wanted. That was a lot of money then. And we also got cash. Yeah, it was a good time I will never forget.

Randall Harris

Sunset Roller Rink, Hamburg

6

SAVAGE SCHOOL

Savage School, Parkdale

The first Parkdale High School, which consolidated with Hamburg School District after the 1993 - 1994 school year, was originally an African American school called Savage High School right outside the town of Parkdale.

According to *The Little Rock Crisis: What Desegregation Politics Says About Us* by R. Perry, in 1958, during the Brown v. Board of Education uproar, the school had twelve teachers and an African American female principal. Jim Johnson, who would later be elected to the Arkansas Supreme Court, was so pro-segregation that he journeyed to multiple schools, including Savage High School, to collect signatures opposing desegregation. Five teachers who refused to be bullied into signing did not have their contracts renewed the following year.

After desegregation, Savage High School was moved to the Parkdale High School site as a 7th through 12th grade location.

> I taught kindergarten there [from around] '86 to '91. One year while I was there a straight line wind came and rolled the roof off the gym. The whole school was in there having recess. There was no kitchen there. The ladies at the high school fixed the lunches and they were brought out to us. We would take the students down the road on a field trip to the graveyard. We would add and subtract the dates to figure how old the people were.
>
> Sandra Oliver

The elementary school operated at Savage School until it eventually closed.
The school, made of two buildings, classrooms and a gym, is now privately owned and monitored, partially used for storage and partially destroyed.

Over the years, teenagers from neighboring towns such as Hamburg, Wilmot, Montrose, Portland, and Lake Village used the building as a place to hang out, calling it "The Pool Hall" because of a pool table in one of the former school rooms. The classroom building is dangerous, especially toward the back where the entire ceiling has caved in and water damaged the inside. The gym itself is still intact and locked.

Savage School, Parkdale

Savage School, Parkdale

Savage School, Parkdale

7

MORRIS BOOKER MEMORIAL COLLEGE

Morris Booker Memorial College, Dermott

The day my nephew and I cruised over to Dermott to look at some of the homes and buildings on the way and in town, we were surprised at how many people stopped to talk to us and ask, "Are you all going to help us?" Our answer was to tell them we would do our best to get the word out about these historic buildings and their dire situations.

That day we stopped at what was several buildings on the campus for Morris Booker Memorial College. The main building, thankfully, is locked and intact, just waiting for a new life. Two of the other structures are not faring so well.

Morris Booker Memorial College has a dual history. Before its final name, the college was the Chicot County Training School in Dermott. The single-story building was built in 1929 by funding from the Rosenwald Fund, a major philanthropic effort to improve educational opportunities for African Americans. It is similar to other schools of the period, with banks of windows providing plentiful light to its seven classrooms. Sometime in the 1940s an auditorium was added to the west side. The building was the second built for the training school with Rosenwald support; the first, a four-room building, was built in 1924 but has not survived.

Morris Booker Memorial College, Dermott

Morris Booker Memorial College, Dermott

The school building is significant as the only surviving Rosenwald-funded school in Chicot County. Its design was based on standard plans developed by Samuel Smith, an agent for the Rosenwald Fund who developed a plan book for various configurations of school buildings, to be used in the fund's work without necessitating the need for an architect for each facility built. The design incorporated an "industrial" room, in which trades could be taught, and the building was sited according to Rosenwald recommendations for the best use of natural lighting. The building served as a public school facility until 1975, after which it was sold to Morris-Booker Memorial College, which was in 2004 using it as a Head Start facility.

The building was listed on the National Register of Historic Places in 2004.

Morris Booker Memorial College, Dermott

Morris Booker Memorial College, Dermott

Morris Booker Memorial College, Dermott

Morris Booker Memorial College, Dermott

Morris Booker Memorial College, Dermott

Morris Booker Memorial College, Dermott

Morris Booker Memorial College, Dermott

8

PLEASANT GROVE CHURCH

So many tiny country churches have quietly existed while the hustle and bustle of the world moves on around them. On a lovely and mild winter day, we stepped through the open door of Pleasant Grove Church in Dermott. Very little furniture remains, although visitors can definitely feel the history of parishioners who once came on Sundays to sing, pray, and listen to the sermon. Although not much history is available on this church, it remains a lovely addition to *Abandoned Arkansas*, as so much of our history is quiet, leaving us to only speculate about the why and the how.

Pleasant Grove Church, Dermott

9

ASHLEY COUNTY NURSING CENTER

Ashley County Nursing Center, Wilmot

In the southern corner of the state, bordering Mississippi and Louisiana, a tiny community quietly sits, still surviving after years of struggle. Wilmot is one of the oldest settlements in eastern Ashley County, although it wasn't incorporated until 1898. Just east of Lake Enterprise, which was once a part of Bayou Bartholomew, Wilmot was a steamboat stop long before the railroad came through, built a depot, and renamed the community. Wilmot sits on Highway 165 between Parkdale (home of the Dr. Williams House and the now defunct Parkdale High School, both featured in this book) and the Louisiana state line.

Ashley County Nursing Center, Wilmot

Ashley County Nursing Center, Wilmot

Ashley County Nursing Center, Wilmot

The Ashley County Nursing Center sits empty and unused on one of the town's long, curving roads through the tiny town. Once a place for residents to spend their twilight years, for nurses and doctors to care for their patients, and for new nurses to train, it is now abandoned. Bed frames and mattresses still remain in the cinderblock rooms. Now, rotting pianos play no more music. The windows still allow beautiful natural light to shine in, but no resident is there to benefit from the glow.

The community of Wilmot has few major businesses left. The elementary school was consolidated with Hamburg School District. EZMart is still bustling, the only stop-and-shop within miles, housing a tiny police station in the same building. Mainline Health Systems (where my mother was a dental hygienist for over twenty years, until she retired in 2018) provided quality medical and dental care for the area residents until its closing in 2019.

Ashley County Nursing Center, Wilmot

10

LAKE VILLAGE COMMERCIAL HISTORIC DISTRICT

The faded sign of "Bee Hive Fashions" is the only real identifying exterior clue of this building (exact dates of operation unknown) which has been abandoned for years, although it remains hanging on, albeit barely, at the end of a block of buildings on the historic Main Street in Lake Village. Relics of its past are still strewn about the store, while parts of the original floor are covered in mud from the collapsed ceiling and balmy delta weather.

The Lake Village Commercial Historic District as a whole encompasses the historic commercial heart of Lake Village, Arkansas, the county seat of Chicot County in the Mississippi River Delta region of southeastern Arkansas. I grew up going to the boat races at the Lake Chicot Water Festival, and my best friend lived on Stuart Island. Lake Village holds a soft spot in my heart; it is close enough to my original hometown of Greenville, Mississippi, yet it is still very Arkansan. The buildings painted bright colors on the square make me particularly happy.

The district covers about six square blocks of downtown Lake Village, bounded roughly by Jackson Street to the north, Lakeshore Drive to the east, Church Street to the south, and Chicot Street to the west. It is this area that truly encompasses the growth of Lake Village during its period of greatest prosperity, roughly between 1906 and 1960, boosted by the railroad in 1903; most of the district's buildings were built between 1900 and 1930. The entire area was listed on the National Register of Historic Places in 2011.

Bee Hive Fashions, Lake Village

11

STRIKER PAPER CORPORATION

Members of our team visited Striker back in 2014. We decided to travel there again one very cold weekend over the Christmas holidays in 2018 in order to do some filming for one of our founder Michael's many projects. It was my first time to the massive industrial time capsule. Anyone who has ever been to Stephens can attest to its remoteness; our cell phones were silent and void of signal. Despite our numb toes, exploring the expanse of this surprisingly bright and varied painted open-air building was as exhilarating as ever. Safety posters, phone bills, giant paper rolls, and scattered bits and bobs told so much about what everyday work life was like at Striker.

In 1956, the plant was constructed and opened as Elk Roofing, a highly profitable business. H. L. Arrington, builder and owner, passed away in 1972; his family sold the plant to the Elk Corporation. The plant continued to do well enough for some time. Sadly, the plant eventually fell upon hard times, leaving it to cease operating due to lack of profit in 1985. It sat, unused until 1991, when Striker Paper Company purchased the facility. The aging building was renovated and refitted with all new factory and production equipment. Soon it was back on track, but only for a little while. Eight years after it reopened, it closed for good. The building continues to sit fenced and unoccupied today just as it has every day since its last closure back in 1998.

Striker Paper Corporation, Stephens

Striker Paper Corporation, Stephens

Striker Paper Corporation, Stephens

Striker Paper Corporation, Stephens

Striker Paper Corporation, Stephens

12

MORE AROUND SOUTH ARKANSAS

Crossett

Above: Crossett

Left: Portland

Above: Hamburg

Right: Dermott

Dermott

Dermott

Aspacia Club, Lake Village

Aspacia Club, Lake Village

Aspacia Club, Lake Village

Portland

Lake Village

Wilmot

Lake Village

Old Greenville Bridge Site, Lake Village

Lake Village

Right: Crossett

Below: Hamburg

Left: Crossett

Below: Lake Village

AFTERWORD

Despite South Arkansas having such small towns, it is absolutely filled with seemingly endless places packed with memories. I have only scratched the surface. What can the everyday person do to help keep these spaces alive? Support funding for historic programs. Help communities raise awareness for places that need help. Ask questions. Get involved with city and state efforts. Even being a member of groups online that celebrate remembering and documenting is helpful.

By buying this book, you've helped. By supporting us on social media, you help. Keep Arkansas and Arkansas history alive by spreading the word. Also, next time you pass a closed-up old house or a long abandoned school, try not to consider it an eyesore; try to think of it as a patient in need of care, if the right resources are used to save it.

Stay curious.

Ginger

ABOUT THE AUTHOR

GINGER BECK is a writer, teacher, urban explorer, and photographer who can't pass up a boarded-up home or abandoned building without craning her neck to get a good, long look and wonder what used to be. Her curiosity and love of history and writing, combined with her craving for adventure and taking photos naturally led to her hobby and obsession of urban and rural exploring with Abandoned Arkansas. She loves her dogs, art, rainstorms, outer space, and dinosaurs. Follow her on instagram @highfiveg.